"This is such a cool ride, and we're having so much fun, we wouldn't give it up for the world."

JOE JONAS to the
Beacon Street Girls website

For Madeleine, the best big sister ever!

Photographs © 2009: AP Images: 31 (Tammie Arroyo), 10, 11 (Mark J. Terrill); **Corbis Images:** back cover, 74 (Mario Anzuoni/Reuters), 97 (Keith Bedford/Reuters), 14, 15, 102 bottom center right, 102 bottom center left, 102 bottom left (Lisa O'Connor/ZUMA); **Getty Images:** 7 right, 60, 61 (Brian Ach), 6 right, 7 left, 66 (Jeff Daly), 50 (James Devaney), 18, 20, 40, 67, 93, 102 bottom right, 103 bottom right, 103 bottom left, 104 center left (Scott Gries), 46 (Frazer Harrison), 83 (Tom Hill), cover main, 2, 3, 72, 81, 82, 85, 86, 87, 94 (Dave Hogan), 52, 53, 98, 99 (Mathew Imaging), 6 left (Jon Kopaloff), 39 right (Sam Levi), 65 (Arnaldo Magnani), 44, 45 (Larry Marano), 1 (Jeffrey Mayer), 56 (Kevin Mazur), 49 (Jamie McCarthy), 84, 90, 91, 104 bottom right (Frank Micelotta), 38, 39 left (Frank Micelotta/Fox), 8, 9, 88 (Ethan Miller), 16 bottom, 17, 27, 33, 34, 35, 36 (Kevin Parry), 78, 79, 103 top right (John Shearer), 62, 63 (Jim Spellman), 71 (Theo Wargo), 23, 24, 28, 29, 43 (Kevin Winter), 12, 13 (Kevin Winter/AMA); **Landov, LLC:** 59 (Jonathan Fickies/Dick Clark Productions), 89 (Roger L. Wollenberg/UPI); **NEWSCOM/Chapple/Beetham/Splash News:** 70; **PacificCoastNews.com/Gaz Shirley:** 69; **Photoshot/Kristin Callahan/Newscom:** 77; **Retna Ltd./Jay Blakesberg:** 54, 55, 57, 104 top right; **ShutterStock, Inc.:** 58 (Barbara Ayrapetyan), 102 top center right (Kellie L. Folkerts), 76 (Marioiram), 104 top left (Adrian Matthiassen), 104 bottom left (Obak), 22 (Alon Othnay), 19 (Massimiliano Pieraccini), 102 top (Sasha Radosavljevich), 16 top (David C. Rehner), 104 center right (Carsten Reisinger), 103 top left (Juha Sompinmäki), 51 (Dmitry Tereshchenko), 102 top center left (TerryM), 103 center (Tramper)

Library of Congress Cataloging-in-Publication Data
Marron, Maggie.
  Jonas Brothers / Maggie Marron.
    p. cm. — (Junk food: tasty celebrity bios)
  Includes bibliographical references, discography, and index.
  Library/Book Clubs/Trade ISBN-10: 0-531-21721-3;
  ISBN-13: 978-0-531-21721-4
  Book Fairs ISBN-10: 0-531-23400-2;
  ISBN-13: 978-0-531-23400-6

  1. Jonas Brothers (Musical group)—Juvenile literature. 2. Rock musicians—United States—Biography—Juvenile literature. I. Title.
  ML3930.J62M37 2009   782.42166092'2—dc22   [B]   2008028312

1 2 3 4 5 6 7 8 9 10 R 18 17 16 15 14 16 12 11 10 09

Jonas

BROTHERS

BY
MAGGIE MARRON

Franklin Watts®
An Imprint of Scholastic Inc.

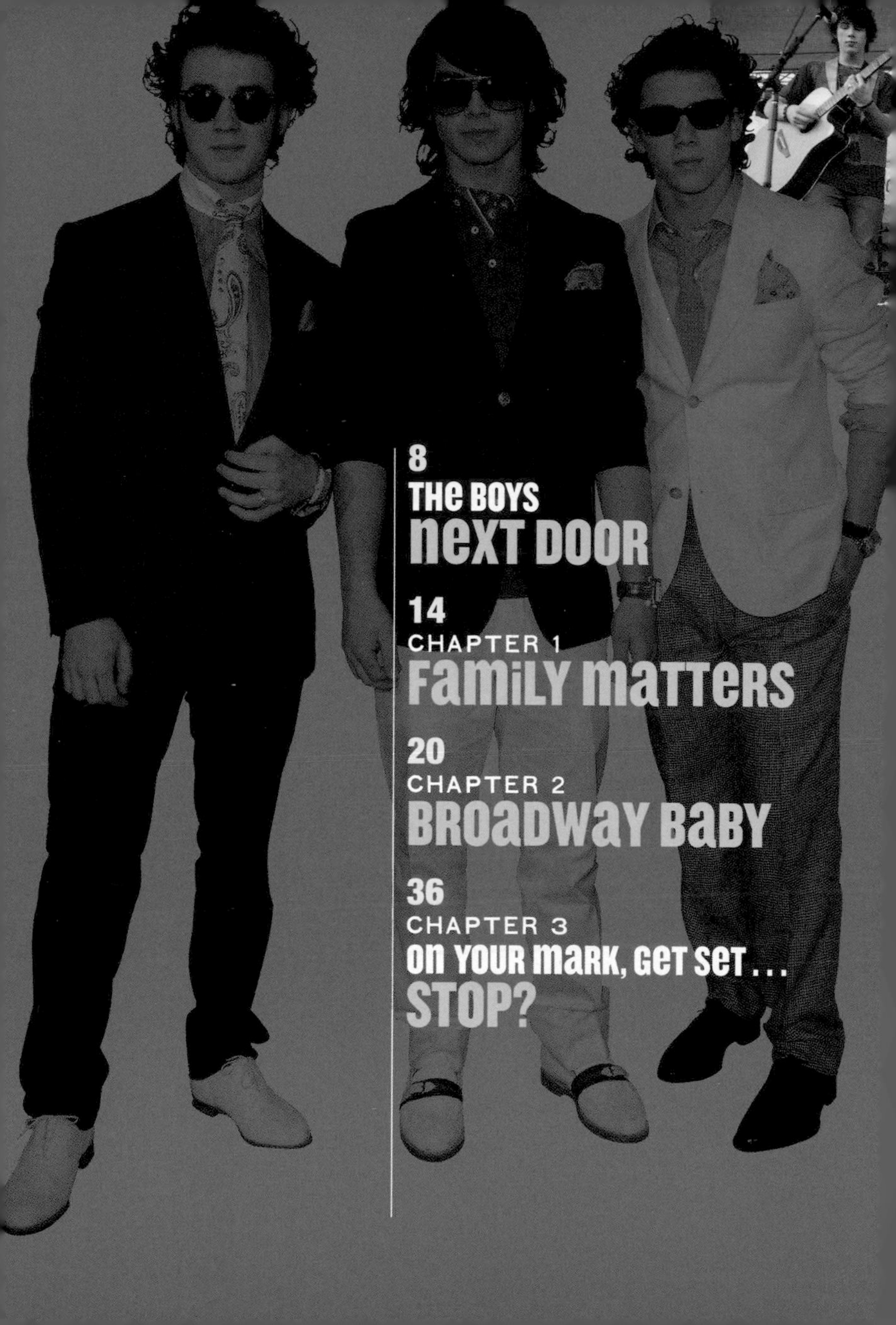

ON THE ROAD
page 66

ALL TOGETHER
page 60

JUNK FOOD

STAR GUiDE

TRIPLE THREAT:
Nick, Joe, and Kevin
Jonas perform at
the 2007 American
Music Awards
in Los Angeles.

THE BOYS NEXT DOOR

You may know them today as the hottest trio of brothers ever to light up a concert stage. And of course you have a favorite—we *all* have a favorite! Their incredible good looks, adorably shaggy locks, and mesmerizing musical talent have helped propel Nick, Joe, and Kevin Jonas from obscurity to superstardom in just a few short years. But the traits you can see and hear are all just icing on a much sweeter cake!

What really makes the Jonas Brothers, well, totally rock, is their special secret weapon. It's one that will keep them

IN TOUCH: Joe reaches out and touches his fans.

soaring while other stars burn out around them. The one that will take them places other musicians can only dream of.

Can you guess what it is?

Flash back to November 18, 2007. The American Music Awards are in full swing. The Jonas Brothers are about to make their grand entrance to perform the heck out of one of their fans'—and their own—favorite songs.

The lights go up. The first notes of "S.O.S." begin to play. In front of where the guys are standing, three glass panes explode, exposing Nick, Joe, and Kevin in all their gorgeous glory. As they dance over the debris, lead singer Joe slips on the broken glass and slices open his hand. Ouch!

Another performer might have freaked out. But not Joe Jonas. Without missing a beat, he pulls himself up, just in time to belt out the very first line of the song. And as fans scream and sing and cry, and then scream some more, the performance goes on without a hitch. "Just a little blood, but, whatever, rock and roll," he explained to *People* magazine, shrugging it off like needing stitches is no biggie.

And, no, he wasn't kidding.

That "whatever" attitude is the Jonas Brothers' secret weapon—a down-to-earth, casual relationship with fame get, they never let any of it get to their heads.

The Jonas Brothers are regular guys. They could be your next-door neighbors. Any one of them could be that kid who sits behind you in chemistry class. And that's what makes them irresistible.

So just who are these super-talented guys next door? Where did they come from—and how did they get where they are today? We're about to serve the whole dish. So sit back, get comfy, and get ready to learn everything there is to know about everyone's favorite band of brothers!

THE SHOW MUST GO ON: Right after the guys took the stage at the 2007 American Music Awards *(opposite page)*, Joe badly cut his hand. He didn't even skip a beat— but just kept on going *(below)*.

JUST GUYS: Sure, they're incredibly famous. Still, the Jonas Brothers don't take themselves too seriously.

FAMILY MATTERS

In the home of the Jonas Brothers, one thing is true: The family that plays together, stays together.

Kevin, Nick, and Joe are for real. Their approachable, attitude-free manner is no act. It's who they are, through and through. And for that they can thank their parents, Kevin and Denise Jonas.

When they met, Kevin and Denise were both musicians based in Teaneck, New Jersey. After they got married, they started a Christian ministry, traveling the country and leading worship programs for the hearing impaired.

Not long after, on November 5, 1987, they welcomed Paul Kevin Jr. into the world. But they didn't let parenthood slow them down. Instead, they bundled up their newborn baby and hit the road.

Less than two years later, the family of three grew to four with the arrival of Joseph Adam, on August 15, 1989. Kevin Sr. and Denise just kept traveling and working, their two tiny boys in tow.

MAMA'S BOYS: The brothers are all really close to their mom.

After a couple more years on the road, Denise got pregnant again. Kevin Sr. and Denise decided to put an end to traveling, and they settled near Dallas, Texas, where Nicholas Jerry was born on November 16, 1992.

We're each other's best friends. People ask us, "Do you guys fight?" But, really, we get along so well.

KEVIN JONAS to
USA Today

JERSEY BOYS

The Jonases liked Texas, but they never felt completely at home there. They decided to go back to their roots and moved the family to Wycoff, New Jersey, about 25 miles from New York City. The brothers now live in Los Angeles, but like other famous Jersey boys— Jon Bon Jovi and Bruce Springsteen—they are proud of the Garden State. At many concerts, they pay tribute to New Jersey, which they call the "Muscle of America." As Joe joked to the *Grand*

MEGASTARS: The Jonas Brothers reach for the stars during a July 2006 concert.

We are good guys. So we don't really use foul language in any of our songs or lives. And we just try to be positive role models. That's just what we do.

NICK JONAS to the
Allentown Morning Call

OVERHEARD

Christmas song that people had heard a million times. He wanted to try to write his own Christmas song.

With help from his musician dad, Nick wrote "Joy to the World (A Christmas Prayer)." By the following year, the song had found its way onto Christian radio stations. So powerful was the piece—and the performer—that Nick was invited to the United Nations in September 2004. There, he sang his song at a ceremony to remember the victims of the September 11, 2001 attacks.

aLL in THe FaMiLY

Within months, Nick got the attention of the Christian record label INO. When he was just 12 years old, the label offered him a contract. Nick was thrilled. He loved writing and singing his own music—especially if it meant collaborating with his dad. And with an entire album to create, he could get the rest of his family involved. Nick, his dad, Kevin, and Joe (with a contribution from Denise) wrote all the words and music for Nick's dazzling debut album, *Nicholas Jonas*. The album will always be important to the Jonas Brothers because it features a special touch from each family member. But little did any of them know that this record, however indirectly, would help launch their hugely successful careers!

Star Faves

COLOR: Blue

DRINK: Orange Gatorade

FOOD: Chicken cutlet sandwich with mayo

CANDY: Twix and Tootsie Rolls

ICE CREAM: Chocolate marshmallow

CEREAL: Trix

FAST FOOD: In-N-Out Burger

SONG: "Only Hope" by Switchfoot

BANDS: Copeland and Switchfoot

TV SHOWS: *Boy Meets World* and *Heroes*

SPORT: Wiffle ball

AUTHOR: Dr. Seuss

BOOK: *A Wrinkle in Time*

CARTOON CHARACTER: Rocko from *Rocko's Modern Life*

BOARD GAME: Monopoly

WORD: Supercalifragilisticexpialidocious

SUBJECTS: Math and physics

JOE!

BONUS

Born September 28, 2000, Franklin Nathaniel Jonas was a late addition to the Jonas family, but he's an important part of it. As the youngest, it's his supreme duty to be the cutest, and he's doing a great job. "Oh, Frankie! Frankie's the man," Joe told *Girls' Life* during the filming of the Disney movie *Camp Rock*. "He owns this set right now. Everybody loves Frankie."

Frankie's just like most other kids his age. He loves riding his bike and watching baseball—especially the New York Yankees. But he's also had his moments in the spotlight. He's been known to jump up onstage with his brothers when fans refuse to stop chanting his name.

JONAS!

There's no doubt about it. Frankie's got the performing bug just as bad as his big brothers. He wants to play the drums when he gets a little older. But if Frankie has his way, he won't settle for joining the Jonas Brothers. He wants a solo career.

His brothers aren't buying it. "He told me he wants to make his own band," Joe said to *Girls' Life*. "So I was like, 'OK, Frankie. All right, fine.'" Talk to us in a few years, Frankie!

In the band or not, Frankie certainly has his own following. "He's really making a name for himself," Kevin told *Newsweek*. "When we do events now, he can't really go anywhere because our fans know him so well they start screaming his name."

THE BOYS IN THE BAND: "I think we would love to be a band that really does last. Because we are brothers, I think it really helps," Joe told the *Seattle Times*.

3

ON YOUR MARK, GET SET... STOP?

The guys get their big break with Columbia Records—but their first album tanks.

When Christmas 2004 arrived, the brothers could be pretty proud of themselves. They had each used their talents to land acting roles. And they'd all helped Nick with his first album.

Still, their careers could have stopped there, if it hadn't been for Steve Greenberg. When Greenberg became president of Columbia Records in January 2005, he had already discovered and launched some pretty serious acts. Ever hear of Hanson, Baha Men, or Joss Stone? Greenberg also earned a Grammy for Best Dance Recording as producer of Baha Men's "Who Let the Dogs Out?" He definitely knew talent when he heard it. So when Nick Jonas's album landed on his desk and he gave it a listen, he was sure he'd just stumbled upon the next big thing.

THaT VOiCe!

Okay, so Greenberg wasn't crazy about the music itself—but that voice! He couldn't stop listening to Nick sing. He hadn't heard such a powerful voice come out of such a young kid since Taylor Hanson. And yes, the Jonas Brothers get the Hanson comparison all the time. Nick, Joe, and Kevin were all big Hanson fans when they

A-LISTERS: Nick, Kevin, and Joe on the red carpet for the 2007 Teen Choice Awards.

	Hanson	**JONAS BROTHERS**
Who's in the band	three brothers	three brothers
Hair	longish blond hair	longish brown hair
Politics	socially conscious	socially conscious
Home state	Oklahoma	New Jersey

side by side

CENTER OF ATTENTION: Jonas fans mob New York City's Times Square in 2006 to catch a glimpse of their favorite rock stars.

were young. Joe, however, feels the need to point out one difference between the Jonases and the Hansons. "We're Italian," he quipped to the *Minneapolis-St. Paul Star Tribune*.

When Greenberg learned that Nick had two brothers who'd helped him create his album, and who jammed regularly with Nick in the family basement, that was all he needed to know. He offered the guys a contract with Columbia.

On THEiR Way?

Kevin and Joe couldn't have been more excited to be taken along for the ride by their little brother. "We never really expected that to happen," Kevin recalled for the *Newark Star-Ledger.* "But once it did, it felt so right."

"Once we started doing this," Nick added, "I realized that that's what it needed to be, because it was just working, and we have so much fun playing together."

The guys had struck gold, and they couldn't wait to turn their magic into platinum—with a platinum record of course. They had signed a significant deal with a major label and had every reason to believe they were on their way. They just had no idea how long it was all going to take.

Itching to get started, the guys wrote song after song. But the executives at Columbia rejected most of them. Soon Columbia hooked them up with some of the top songwriters in the business, and they finally put the album together. But even with the professional help, executives at the label didn't like the music. They kept sending the guys back to the drawing board to create new tunes. For Nick, Joe, and Kevin, it was an exhausting process. And as far as they could tell, the label didn't have any real plans to publicize and promote the band. The guys were starting to wonder why they'd ever been signed in the first place.

iT'S aBOUT TiMe!

The Jonas Brothers decided to call their debut album *It's About Time,* not because it took them so long to complete (OK, so maybe that was part of it), but because most of the songs have to do with time. There's "Time for Me to Fly," "Year 3000," (covered from the British band Busted), "One Day at a Time," "6 Minutes," (covered from Lyte Funky Ones), and "7:05."

When the band finished recording, the studio still wasn't ready to release the album. To get exposure and build a fan base, the brothers hit the road. They toured with Avril Lavigne, Menudo, and other top acts and drummed up excitement wherever they played. "We played everywhere and played anything we could," Kevin recalled for the *New Haven Register.* "We were playing shows, just trying to do the rock 'n' roll band thing, make it happen."

By December 2005, it seemed that the brothers were well on their way to making it happen. They released their first single, "Mandy," which became a huge hit on *TRL*.

S.O.S.

Unfortunately, the success of "Mandy" didn't translate into record sales. When Columbia finally released *It's About Time* on August 8, 2006, it flopped big time, selling a mere 62,000 copies. And if that wasn't bad enough, Greenberg, the band's main supporter, left Columbia. Around Christmas of 2006, with their strongest advocate out of the picture, the Jonas Brothers were dropped by Columbia.

The guys were devastated.

DiD YOU KNOW?

"MANDY" WAS INSPIRED BY A REAL PERSON. She is a family friend (and former girlfriend of Joe's) named Mandy Vandamye, who learned sign language from their mom. Look for her in all three versions of the "Mandy" video!

Here it was, just before Christmas, and they'd just been royally Scrooged. As Joe recalled for *Entertainment Weekly*, "I remember thinking: Oh, this really stinks. Is this the end of our beginning career?"

With a huge dark cloud of disappointment and rejection hanging over their heads, they hardly could have known that this was only the beginning.

SETTING THE STAGE: The Jonas Brothers perform as Jesse McCartney's opening act in Boca Raton, Florida, in April 2007.

HOLD ON! It's been a wild ride for the Jonas Brothers. Here they strike a pose at Nickelodeon's 2006 Kids' Choice Awards.

HOORaY FOR HOLLYWOOD

A new label signs the Jonas Brothers and propels them to their most incredible year yet.

Although the Jonas family was disappointed during the 2006 holiday season, they stayed positive. And it didn't take long for their optimism to pay off. In February 2007, Hollywood Records contacted the Jonas Brothers and signed them to the label. Not a bad New Year's gift.

If you don't know who Hollywood Records is, here's a clue. They're the record label for a company you may have heard of—Disney! Other careers they've launched? How about Miley Cyrus, The Cheetah Girls, Hilary Duff, Jordan Pruitt—and the list goes on! So not only were the guys being given a second chance, they were now in the hands of an even bigger, more powerful company than the one that had given up on them.

"THAT'S JUST THE WAY WE ROLL"

If Columbia had crept like a snail to get the guys' first record out, Hollywood sprinted like a cheetah (that would be the fastest land animal in the world). Hollywood understood what a prize they had and didn't take it for granted. On August 7, 2007, the label released *Jonas Brothers*, and the album debuted at number five on the Billboard Top 200 charts. "By the time we were on Hollywood," Nick told *Entertainment Weekly*, "we made the record that we really wanted to make." Unlike *It's About Time*, almost every track on *Jonas Brothers* was written by Nick, Joe, and Kevin.

Songs from that album include "S.O.S.," "That's Just the Way We Roll," and "When You Look Me in the Eyes." Soon the songs were burning up the request lines at *Total Request Live* and breaking records for downloads on iTunes. YouTube viewers watched their videos millions of times.

IN PERSON: Nick, Joe, and Kevin relax between songs at the MTV studios in New York City.

WE'LL BE BACK: Kevin and Joe head home after an episode of *Total Request Live*.

With a couple of their songs included on various film and TV soundtracks—plus small TV appearances on *Zoey 101*, the Cartoon Network's *Fridays*, and other shows—the guys were starting to make their presence felt.

meeting miley

So with all this Jonas buzz crackling around, you can guess that it didn't take long for the producers of Miley Cyrus's smash hit show *Hannah Montana* to notice. In the summer of 2007, the brothers starred in a *Hannah* episode created and named just for them!

In "Me and Mr. Jonas and Mr. Jonas and Mr. Jonas," Miley Cyrus's character, Miley Stewart, gets totally annoyed when her dad, Robby, agrees to write songs for the Jonas Brothers. Everything eventually works out, and Miley, her dad, and the Jonas Brothers all rock out to "We Got the Party" at the end.

The episode was a blast for

T or F

Joe says if he could live in any past era, it would be the 1920s.

FALSE! He would love to live in the 1960s or 1970s.

everyone involved. It was fun to film, and the chemistry between Miley and the guys really came through. Later that year, the Jonases presented Miley with Nickelodeon's 2007 Kids' Choice Award for "Favorite TV Actress," and Miley gave the guys the credit they deserved. "They were amazing!" she yelled to the screaming audience. (The very next year, the guys would win their own Kids' Choice Award, for "Favorite Music Group"!)

The brothers were so amazing, in fact, that they got an invite to join Miley on her *Best of Both Worlds* tour. And what a tour it was! Starting on October 18, 2007, in St. Louis, the Jonas Brothers were on the road for about three months with Miley and her crew. They played more than 50 dates and

OFFSTAGE FUN:
The Jonases and
Miley Cyrus hang
out at Six Flags.

stole the hearts of millions of fans. Many concertgoers who had come to the shows to see Miley got their first dose of the Jonas Brothers live—and loved it!

WRiTiNG aND RiDiNG

On their whirlwind tour with Miley, the brothers had little time to relax. They

STAR STATS

MILEY CYRUS

BORN: November 23, 1992

BIRTH NAME: Destiny Hope Cyrus

SIGN: Sagittarius

HOMETOWN: Thompson's Station, Tenn.

SIBLINGS: Noah (sister), Braison (brother), Brandi (half sister), Christopher Cody (half brother), Trace (half brother)

FAVORITE SPORT: Cheerleading

FAVORITE COLORS: Lime green and pink

FAVORITE ALBUM: *Breakaway* by Kelly Clarkson

FAVORITE MOVIE: *Steel Magnolias*

FAVORITE BOOK: *Don't Die, My Love,* by Lurlene McDaniel

BEST OF BOTH WORLDS:
The Jonas Brothers and Miley
Cyrus got together for the
must-see tour of 2007.

crisscrossed the country to perform in sold-out shows in huge arenas. Between shows, they spent long hours on the tour bus traveling from city to city—but they didn't waste a minute. Cruising down the open highway, the guys wrote and actually began recording their third album. Talk about energy!

Although this wasn't the most conventional way to produce songs, Hollywood was firmly behind them. "The bus thing isn't necessarily ideal," Hollywood VP Jon Lind told *Billboard* magazine. "But the guys are in the absolute most creative period of their careers, and the music is pouring out of them."

Gossip Alert!

Did Nick date Miley? It depends whom you ask. The *New York Post* and other publications will swear that he did briefly. But many online sources say it's not true.

SHARING THE STAGE:
Miley Cyrus introduced zillions of Hannah/Miley fans to the Jonas Brothers.

The brothers totally agreed. "With this next record, it was just more of an evolution of who we are," Kevin explained to the *Fort Worth Star-Telegram*. "We grew up a little bit. We wrote some deeper songs and experimented with new instruments."

CENTER STAGE

At the end of the year, the Jonas Brothers got a chance to take their new, grown-up sound on the road—as the headline act. They were still on tour with Miley when

T or F

?

Joe can't live without coffee.

FALSE!
He's totally a tea guy!

they got the opportunity. Live Nation, an events company known for signing huge names like Madonna, the Police, and the Rolling Stones, decided to take a chance on the rookie rockers. The tour promoters offered the band a two-year deal!

The brothers are still scratching their heads over it. "In a weird way, it's humbling," Nick told the Associated Press. "People think you'd get a big head about it, but it's like, 'Wow. Someone would do this?'"

Nick, Joe, and Kevin had mixed feelings about leaving Miley because they loved working with her. "Miley and all of her people are just really fun and awesome to be around," Nick said to the *Las Vegas Review Journal*. "But we're really excited to go on our own tour and play our songs . . . and be able to connect with our fans."

BLACK TIE: The Jonases and Miley helped ring in the New Year at Times Square in 2007.

TAKING OFF: 2007 was a phenomenal—and frazzling—year for the Jonas Brothers.

ON THE ROAD

What a year 2007 was for the band—and what a challenge for the tight-knit Jonas family.

As soon as tickets for their *Look Me in the Eyes* tour went on sale, the guys began breaking records for sold-out shows. By the end of 2007, their faces—and their songs—were everywhere. They performed at the American Music

Awards, at the Macy's Thanksgiving Day Parade, and on Dick Clark's famous New Year's Eve show. More than ten million people had watched their *Hannah Montana* episode. Millions more saw them every week in TV ads for Baby Bottle Pop candy. Their videos on YouTube were drawing more than a million hits each.

In just over three years, the Jonas Brothers had come a long way from their basement jam sessions. They had also put their family values and their regular-guy personalities to the test.

> **We remember a year ago; we were in a van, and that's how we traveled, no buses, no trucks, or anything. It was kind of just starting from the ground up. Now we have a sold-out tour; it's really exciting.**
>
> **KEVIN JONAS**
> to the *Evansville Courier*

OVERHEARD!

NEXT QUESTION? Kevin, Joe, and Nick in the press room at Madison Square Garden in New York City in 2007.

MISSING THE PROM

Touring presented a huge challenge to the family. Before the deal with Columbia, the brothers all attended school every day, no matter what acting projects they had on the side. When they started touring, school became impossible. The boys—including Frankie—were all home- (or bus-) schooled so the family wouldn't have to split up while the band was on the road.

Missing school did have its downsides—most of which the brothers were able to shrug off. "Sometimes it's like, 'Man, I'm not going to go to prom,'" Joe told the *Newark Star-Ledger*. "You think about it for like five seconds, and then the five seconds is over, because you're like, 'No one else is doing what I'm doing, at my age,' which is such a blessing."

The brothers also feel blessed by their late-night hours. They've each confessed that the worst part about going to a regular school was having to get up so early in the morning.

In addition to prom night, the boys also had to say good-bye to their privacy. They have trouble going out without attracting a crowd. Even early on, when they still played small venues, it was hard to get a moment's peace.

LiFe in a FiSHBOWL

In an interview with the *New York Post*, Nick recalled one close encounter with an army of eager fans at a school show. "I was chilling backstage, when all of a sudden the doors—which I thought were locked—burst open and 30 girls came and tackled me," he said. Not that he's really complaining. "Thirty girls against one little dude. It was rough, but not the worst thing in the world."

Joe remembers his share of semi-scary memories, too. "We've had some interesting situations with some fans . . . ones that will just come up and almost jump on you and be like, 'I love you, I love you!'" he told *Details*. "It's kind of awkward when they're like, 'Oh, you're so hot!' How do you say anything to that?"

Kevin, the ladies' man, seems to take all this "fan-demonium" in stride better than his brothers. In more

OVER HERE! Kevin pauses to sign an autograph as he and Joe push through the paparazzi in New York City in 2007.

AT THE MALL? Nick, Joe, and Kevin perform an acoustic number at a mall in Boca Raton, Florida.

than one city, he's been known to visit fans waiting in ticket lines, bringing them coffee and donuts—and a huge helping of Jonas love!

NICK'S SCARE

The band got a real scare on the road near the end of 2005. Nick had been feeling tired all the time. He was always thirsty and was losing lots of weight. His parents took him to the doctor's, where he was diagnosed with diabetes. Skinny, thirsty, and run-down, Nick was terrified. "Am I going to die?" he asked the doctor.

The answer was a definite "no." But managing diabetes while on the road has proved challenging. Nick has to check his blood sugar several times a day. When he was first diagnosed, he gave himself daily shots of insulin, a hormone that helps his body process sugar. With paparazzi following the band at all hours, there was always a chance that a photo of Nick sticking a needle in his arm would surface, along with a story claiming that he has a drug problem. Now he carries a device under his clothes that automatically injects him when he needs an insulin boost.

Nick takes his diabetes in stride. He also uses his fame to give people with diabetes a share of the spotlight. In March 2007, the brothers played a benefit for diabetes research, and Nick told the crowd—and the world—about his life with the disease. "Everyone has a story about how they manage their diabetes," Nick told the *Star-Ledger.* "I'm just a kid from New Jersey who is able to share my story."

MAKING A DIFFERENCE: Nick has used his celebrity to raise awareness about diabetes.

Somehow, even as they become internationally known stars, the brothers still see themselves exactly that way: They're just regular guys from New Jersey. On the road or at home, they try to

DID YOU KNOW?

KEVIN BELIEVES IN LOVE AT FIRST SIGHT.

keep their lives as normal as possible. As Kevin told the *Richmond Times-Dispatch*, "We try to go to malls. We try to hang out. We have good friends. We work a lot, but we enjoy our time." And that means having fun wherever they can find it—even at "work." "We'll have an entire arena become our playground," he added. "We turn it into a Wiffle-ball stadium, and we're pitching to each other and [having] home-run derbies. It's pretty amazing."

STAYiNG GROUNDED

The brothers get their easygoing attitude primarily from one source: their family. "We have a really strong family base, and that plays a big role in staying grounded," Nick said to the *Seattle Times*. He says they all stay humble and keep level heads.

The Jonases make the most of the time they spend together. They laugh a lot and goof around—and they also do a lot of bonding. In one of the behind-the-scenes clips from their April 24, 2008, appearance on *Oprah*, the family is seen having a low-key, room-service breakfast together, talking about their crazy tour schedule for the week, but still connecting and sharing plenty of laughs. And that's pretty much how it goes with them.

If the boys ever get too obsessed with careers, they have their parents to set them straight. Both Denise and Kevin Sr. are determined to keep their kids from giving in to the temptations of easy money and overnight fame. "We're not raising boys," Kevin Sr. explained to *People* magazine.

LAZY SUNDAY: Joe and Nick take their brother Frankie out for a ride during a brief break from touring in 2008.

"We're raising men and fathers and husbands. It's very important to us that they can live their dreams, but the first priority is that they're good people."

LV, KJ: Kevin takes a moment to send a text message.

WHAT a CHORE

In part, that means no easy ride for the brothers at home. All the Jonas kids, including the internationally known stars, are expected to do chores and follow the law of the land. "Just because we play music doesn't mean our parents aren't going to discipline us," Nick explained to the *New York Post*. "They do not mind grounding us from our cell phones and TV—not me too much, because I'm a good kid, but Kevin and Joe get their cell phones grounded almost every day, just for being stupid, I guess, not taking out the trash or washing dishes."

Has their newfound fame sparked fighting in the family? Joe admitted to *USA Today* that he and his brothers are prone to "bickering over small things, like who's going to play video games first when we get to a venue."

TOUGH TICKET: The brothers perform at New York City's Madison Square Garden in December 2007.

GOOD TIMES: Kevin and Nick share a laugh before a 2008 gig in London.

But when it comes down to it, they don't have time to fight. "You get onstage every night and you play a concert, so you can't really start arguing and throwing guitars at each other," Joe told the Beacon Street Girls website. "If we ever do have any little arguments, it's usually about the smallest things, the smallest details: What song are we going with? Or why is Nick wearing my socks? Stuff like that."

"it's ReaLLy a LoT oF Fun"

That's not to deny that the brothers get competitive with each other, especially when it comes to—that's right—girls. Joe told *USA Today* about his favorite gripe: "Sometimes you see a very pretty girl in the audience, and you think, 'I hope she's a fan of me.' Then you realize that she's Nick's fan—because she's holding a sign that says, 'Nick, look at me,' or 'Nick, I'm your wife and you just don't know it.' And you're like, 'Oh, bummer.'"

That is about as uptight as the Jonases seem to get about their careers. Never mind that they have a schedule busier than that of many CEOs. Never mind that their tour promoter and their record label have invested millions in them. Never mind that night after night they have to please thousands of fans. "There's not really a lot of pressure," Joe told the *Washington Times*. "Not much at all. It's really a lot of fun."

The fun continued through the first half of 2008. The *Look Me in the Eyes* tour ended March 22, 2008, after 39 sold-out shows. Before the guys had time to put their feet up, their summer tour was announced. *Burning Up* was set to kick off in Toronto on July 4, 2008. Before that, it was off to Europe for 16 shows in June. So much for having a summer vacation!

WISE GUYS: The Jonas Brothers make their entrance at Nickelodeon's 2008 Kids' Choice Awards in Los Angeles.

LIVIN' THE DREAM

With a tour behind them, and a new tour and album on the way, do the Jonas Brothers really have time to give back? You betcha!

Throughout their rise to superstardom, the Jonas Brothers have lived by this mantra: "Remember the Dream." It's all about staying committed to their values. That means that the more good fortune their success brings to them, the more they try to give something back to the world.

T or F

?

Joe's favorite animals are giraffes.

Joe loves monkeys!

FALSE!

WALKING THE WALK

No matter how busy they get, the brothers make time to play benefit concerts whenever they can. Since Nick's diagnosis, they've raised thousands of dollars for diabetes research. They've auctioned off everything from autographed t-shirts to backstage meetings to locks of hair for charities. In October 2007, they played a 900-seat auditorium in Florida to help a local elementary school build a playground for children with special needs.

Every year since the Disney Channel Games started in 2006, the guys have competed in this week-long event. In Orlando, Florida, contestants endure grueling competitions—like posing as pieces on a giant foosball table or matching fellow stars with their baby pictures. All proceeds for the televised event are donated to charity.

In addition to the work they do as a group, each of the guys is involved in his own special charitable efforts. Each brother gives at least ten percent of his earnings to charity—and then some! Kevin has traveled to Mexico and Indonesia to help build hospitals, schools, and churches. And Nick still runs the Nicholas Jonas Change for the Children Foundation, which he started when he was ten years old. It's a nonprofit organization devoted to the needs of abused, homeless, and seriously ill children.

The boys trace a lot of their charitable impulse to their

GIVING BACK:
The Jonases make an appearance at a Special Olympics function in New York City.

NATIONAL TREASURE: The Jonas Brothers—performing here at the Walt Disney Studios in 2008—have become one of America's top bands.

religious faith, which is firmly rooted in their upbringing. "Thankfully, it's almost like we have a pastor with us all the time since our dad is an ordained minister," Joe explained to the *World Entertainment News Network*.

In addition, all three of the brothers wear purity rings. "[We've made] promises to ourselves and to God that we'll stay pure till marriage," Joe added.

DiD YOU KNOW?

DISNEY'S 25TH ANNIVERSARY DOUBLE-DISC DVD OF *THE JUNGLE BOOK* features the guys' totally rockin' cover of "I Wanna Be Like You." (The single also appears on *DisneyMania 5*.)

FanS FiRST

Nick, Joe, and Kevin take their commitments seriously. And they are firmly committed to the people who have made their success possible. (That would be us—their fans!) Back in 2007, when they toured with Miley Cyrus, they felt that a lot of devoted fans were disappointed. Outside companies called ticket brokers were accused of buying up tickets to Miley's concerts and reselling them at much higher prices. The brothers vowed that if they ever got a chance to headline a tour, they would try to even the score with the ticket brokers.

Before the *Look Me in the Eyes* tour, the brothers came up

GLOBE-TROTTER: Kevin gets in his licks at a concert outside of London, England.

VOICE OF GOLD: Lead singer Joe holds the band together with his powerful vocals.

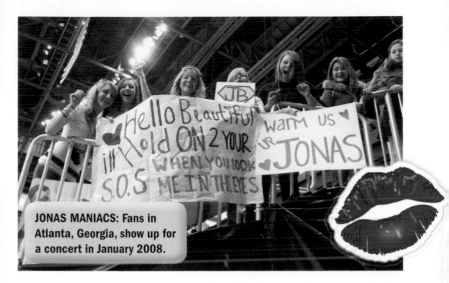

JONAS MANIACS: Fans in Atlanta, Georgia, show up for a concert in January 2008.

with a plan to give great seats to their most devoted fans—at reasonable prices. They held a ticket lottery for seats in the first 20 rows. Fans had to stand in line to get a lottery number. If their numbers fell within a certain range, they got to see the band up close and personal. This lottery kept the ticket brokers out by limiting the number of tickets each lottery-winner could buy.

Obviously, the brothers couldn't accommodate all the thousands of fans who waited in line, but they truly did their best. "We wanted our real fans to be right up front so we can play and get the energy from them rather than having some really rich cats [sitting there]," Joe explained to the Associated Press.

To thank their fans for their devotion, the band has also been known to play free shows at radio stations, in parking lots, and in other places where fans have gathered. When tickets went on sale for their show at the Nokia Theatre, outside of Dallas, Texas, the guys played a free, surprise show for fans freezing in line. Adoring onlookers were treated to a performance of "Year 3000," which the Jonas Brothers performed from the roof of the box office in the January cold. If that's not love, what is?

SURPRISE! The brothers give an impromptu performance for fans waiting to buy tickets for the 2008 show in Dallas.

DRIVING FORCE: Nick's professionalism and ambition got the band its start.

THE JET SET: The Jonas Brothers exit a private jet on their way to a concert in London.

7

KiDS OF THE FUTURE

Can the Jonas Brothers beat the odds and make a lasting mark on the world of show business? At the start of the *Burning Up* tour in the summer of 2008, the brothers were on top of the world. Their tour dates quickly sold out, and they added several more. Their new album, *A Little Bit Longer*, was scheduled to hit stores in August. "It's going to be a fun record," Kevin told *USA Today*. "Everyone keeps asking us, 'What's the attitude? What should we be looking for?' I'd say it's a hopeful, good-time kind of record. It brings a smile to our faces."

In the spring, the band seemed to be everywhere. You could turn on the TV at any time during the day or night and catch a glorious glimpse. There were the two songs they performed on a results show of *Dancing With the Stars*. There was a late-night appearance on *Jimmy Kimmel*. And in April, *Oprah* devoted half a show to the brothers and their family.

> **Watch the mistakes of the people you admire the most, and don't make those mistakes.**
>
> **NICK CARTER** of the Backstreet Boys, giving advice to the Jonas Brothers

After such a dizzying ride to the top, you have to ask, what does the future hold for these guys? A lot of teen stars burn bright for a short time and then disappear from the sky. Some fall victim to drugs. Others simply can't figure out how to draw an older audience as they grow into their twenties and beyond. Can the Jonases thrive in the pressure-cooker of *Billboard* charts, endless road trips, and prying paparazzi?

OVERHEARD

SEAL OF APPROVAL: The Jonas Brothers earned a trip to the White House in 2008.

Jonases in the White House

No one can predict the future, but all the signs point in the right direction. First of all, the guys have the support and encouragement of a level-headed family. Denise and Kevin Sr. taught their kids to think long-term, not short-term. Their desire to raise "good people" rather than millionaire celebrities is bound to help the boys make good decisions down the road. "My mom always told us, 'I'm [teaching you manners] for when you sit at the president's table,'" Joe told *Details* magazine.

LOOK ME IN THE EYES:
The Jonases onstage in
Tucson, Arizona, in 2008.

Who could have predicted that training would come in handy? U.S. President George Bush and First Lady Laura Bush invited the guys to the White House several times. When the brothers went to the annual White House Press Dinner in April 2008, they seemed to need more security than the president himself. "It's crazy," Nick said to *People* magazine of the fan frenzy that erupted when they arrived. "We never expected this."

To supplement the good management they get at home, the brothers have talented professionals to guide their careers. "We have a really good . . . management team," Nick told the *New Haven Register*. "And they've done a very good job of making sure that we have enough time for the projects that we want to do."

ON THE SMALL SCREEN

A lot of those projects showcase the brothers' broad range of talents by drawing on their acting experience from way back. In June 2008, they starred in *Camp Rock*, their very own made-for-TV Disney movie. The guys play members of a band called Connect Three. They're working as celebrity counselors at a camp for aspiring musicians when they make an incredible discovery—and help a talented, hardworking girl land the big break she's always dreamed of. Originally, Disney wanted just Joe to be in the movie but then decided it would be a much better film if all the guys were involved. Thank goodness for that!

In the fall of 2008, they added to their acting resume with a series called *J.O.N.A.S.!* (*Junior Operatives Networking As Spies*). In it, the guys play high-school students who also happen to be musicians—but there's more to this band than meets the eye. These aspiring rock stars also work for the government, moonlighting as spies.

CAMP ROCK: Nick, Joe, and Kevin at the premiere for *Camp Rock*, their 2008 feature film.

We go through things that people in college, high school, middle school, and even older people can relate to. We write songs that mean something to us about what we're going through, and people understand what we're talking about.

KEVIN JONAS to the *Orlando Sentinel*

OVERHEARD!

In two other screen projects, the brothers play the most alluring characters of all: themselves. Their reality TV show, *Jonas Brothers: Living the Dream*, gave their fans a revealing look behind the scenes at life on a Jonas Brothers tour. Then came their debut on the big screen—in the 3D concert film of the *Burning Up* tour.

LOOKiNG aHEaD

So how do the guys feel about acting on film versus performing live shows? "[It's] much easier than being onstage," Joe told *Grand Central Magazine*, "because if you mess up a line, you can say, 'Cut,' and start over." Not exactly something you can get away with live!

Acting is definitely important to the brothers, especially Nick, who would have been perfectly happy to spend his career on the Broadway stage. To this day, Nick still misses the theater. His time on Broadway, he says, helped him feel comfortable performing in front of huge audiences. "Broadway was really great training for what we're doing now," he told the *Minneapolis–St. Paul Star Tribune*. But would he ever sign up for another play? Not likely. "I love being in a band with my brothers," he says.

For Kevin and Joe, as well as Nick, the music is the first priority. "I think we would love to be a band that really does last," Joe told the *Seattle Times*. "Because we are brothers, I think it really helps."

It also doesn't hurt that since day one, they've been serious about their musical training. "We're not a choreographed dance group. And we write our own songs, perform our songs, and play all our instruments," Kevin explained to the *St. Louis Post-Dispatch*. "That shows who we are as people, and it's another way for people to connect with us."

THE BROTHERS COME FIRST

But what happens if they get tired of singing in a new city every night? What else might the future have in store? "We hope to be writing for other artists and producing for other people," Kevin told the *Orlando Sentinel*. But he doesn't rule out the possibility that they could be hitting the stage well into the next decade—and even decades after that, like the Rolling Stones. "Maybe we'll end up touring and making music for years to come," he says.

One thing's for sure: Whatever they do, they're going to do it together! "Opportunities will come along the way," Joe told the *Allentown Morning Call*. "But we all know that even if, say, we want to start side projects for different bands . . . the Jonas Brothers comes first for us."

STAR GUIDE

Think you know everything about the guys? Keep reading!

STAR STATS

NAMES:
Paul Kevin Jr., Joseph Adam, and Nicholas Jerry

ALSO KNOWN AS:
Kevin, Joe, and Nick

HOMETOWN:
Teaneck, NJ (even though Joe was born in Arizona, and Nick in Texas)

LITTLE BROTHER:
Franklin Nathaniel

FRANKIE'S BAND:
Webline

PARENTS:
Kevin and Denise Jonas

SCHOOL:
They're all homeschooled.

RECORD LABEL:
Hollywood Records

FIRST BIG HIT:
"Mandy," in December 2005

% OF INCOME THEY GIVE TO CHARITY: 10%

NAME OF TOUR BUS:
Bertha

NUMBER OF GUITARS THEY OWN:
29. Kevin has 12, Joe has 5, and Nick has 12.

STAR STATS

BIRTH DATE:
August 15, 1989

BIRTHPLACE:
Casa Grande, Arizona

FAVORITE COLOR: Blue

FAVORITE FOOD: Chicken cutlet sandwich

FAVORITE SONG:
"Only Hope" by Switchfoot

FAVORITE BANDS:
Copeland and Switchfoot

FAVORITE ACTORS:
Jim Carrey and
Natalie Portman

FAVORITE MOVIE:
Dumb and Dumber

JOE!

KEVIN!

BIRTH DATE:
November 5, 1987

BIRTHPLACE: Teaneck,
New Jersey

FAVORITE COLOR:
Forest green

FAVORITE FOOD: Sushi

FAVORITE SONG: "3x5"
by John Mayer

FAVORITE MUSICIAN:
John Mayer

FAVORITE ACTORS:
James Dean and
Rachel McAdams

BIRTH DATE: September 16, 1992

BIRTHPLACE: Dallas, Texas

FAVORITE COLOR: Blue

FAVORITE FOOD: Steak

FAVORITE SONG: "Superstition" by Stevie Wonder

FAVORITE BAND: Switchfoot

FAVORITE ACTORS: Matt Long and Keri Lynn Pratt

FAVORITE MOVIE: *Finding Neverland*

FAVORITE TV SHOWS: *Lost* and *SportsCenter*

NICK!

FAVORITE MOVIE: *About a Boy*

FAVORITE TV SHOW: *Close to Home*

FAVORITE SPORT: Pole-vaulting

POP QUIZ

You've read
the book—
now take
the quiz.

1. **When Joe cut his hand on broken glass during the 2007 American Music Awards, he . . .**
   a) kept right on singing
   b) fainted
   c) asked whether there was a doctor in the house
   d) didn't notice

2. **The Jonas brothers grew up in . . .**
   a) New York
   b) Georgia
   c) Connecticut
   d) none of the above

3. **The Jonases were born in which order?**
   a) Kevin, Nick, Joe, Frankie
   b) Nick, Kevin, Frankie, Joe
   c) Kevin, Joe, Nick, Frankie
   d) Joe, Kevin, Nick, Frankie

4. **Nick was discovered at . . .**
   a) a shopping mall
   b) a barbershop
   c) a restaurant
   d) church

5. **Nick's first role on the New York stage was . . .**
   a) Chip in *Beauty and the Beast*
   b) Young Simba in *The Lion King*
   c) Gavroche in *Les Misérables*
   d) Tiny Tim in *A Christmas Carol*

6. **Kevin's favorite subjects in school are . . .**
   a) Latin, history, physical science, and chemistry
   b) biology, art, English, and French
   c) Spanish, geometry, history, and gym
   d) physical science, music, Latin, and theater

7. **Joe has always wanted to be a . . .**
a) TV talk-show host
b) veterinarian
c) comedian
d) restaurant owner

8. **The Jonas Brothers song "Mandy" is actually named after . . .**
a) their grandmother
b) their pet ferret
c) a dog they had when they were little
d) a former girlfriend of Joe's

9. **The Jonas Brothers began writing and recording their third album . . .**
a) while on vacation in Hawai'i
b) while traveling from city to city on a tour bus
c) while on a meditative retreat
d) while holed up in their hotel room between shows

10. **Throughout their rise to superstardom, the Jonas brothers have lived by this mantra . . .**
a) "Less Is More"
b) "Live in the Moment!"
c) "Jonas Brothers Rule!"
d) "Remember the Dream"

11. **Kevin has shown his appreciation for his fans by . . .**
a) bringing them coffee and donuts while they stand in line for tickets
b) tossing hundreds of free tickets out the window of the Jonas Brothers' hotel room
c) volunteering to cook a meal for ten lucky fans chosen at random
d) breaking into song upon request while at the grocery store

12. **To raise money for charity, the Jonas Brothers have auctioned off . . .**
a) locks of their hair
b) doodles that they've drawn
c) old stinky sneakers that they've worn
d) their first instruments

TIMELINE

BAH, HUMBUG !!!

Christmas 2002 Nick writes and sings his own Christmas song on a Broadway holiday album.

1999 Nick is discovered in a New Jersey barbershop, gets an agent, and lands his first Broadway role—as Tiny Tim in *A Christmas Carol.*

November 2003 Nick's song "Joy to the World (A Christmas Prayer)" gets widespread attention on Christian radio stations.

Fall 2004 Christian record label INO signs Nick to a record deal.

September 16, 1992 Nicholas Jerry Jonas is born.

START HERE

November 5, 1987 Paul Kevin Jonas Jr. is born.

August 15, 1989 Joseph Adam Jonas is born.

August 2007 The brothers guest star on *Hannah Montana*. Their album *Jonas Brothers* is released.

March 2007 The brothers play a benefit for diabetes research, and Nick reveals that he has the disease.

Early 2005 Steve Greenberg hears Nick's single "Dear God" and signs the three brothers as a group act.

February 2007 Hollywood Records signs the Jonas Brothers.

August 2006 First album, *It's About Time*, finally comes out—and flops.

Late 2005 After a year of touring and recording, the brothers' first single, "Mandy," is released. Nick is diagnosed with diabetes.

October 2007
The brothers go on tour with Miley Cyrus.

January 2008
The brothers kick off the Look Me in the Eyes tour, their first as a headline act.

June 2008
Camp Rock airs on the Disney Channel.

May 2008
Jonas Brothers: Living the Dream airs on the Disney Channel.

ON THE AIR

July 2008 The boys kick off their Burning Up tour.

August 2008
The Jonas Brothers' third album, *A Little Bit Longer*, is released.

awards

Nickelodeon Kids' Choice Awards, 2008
"Favorite Music Group"

What Perez Sez on VH1, 2007
"Hottest Teen Sensation of 2007"

Discography

ALBUMS
Jonas Brothers [Bonus Tracks], 2008
A Little Bit Longer, 2008
Jonas Brothers: Karaoke, 2008
Jonas Brothers, 2007
It's About Time, 2006

SINGLES
"**Burnin' Up**," 2008
"**S.O.S.**," 2008
"**Hold On**," 2007
"**Year 3000**," 2007
"**Mandy**," 2005

TOURS

The Burning Up Tour, 2008
The Best Damn Tour, 2008
The Look Me in the Eyes Tour, 2008
The Best of Both Worlds Tour, 2007–2008
Marvelous Party Tour, 2007
American Club Tour, 2006

FiLMS anD TeLeViSiOn SeRieS

J.O.N.A.S.!, 2008
Camp Rock, 2008

FAN SITES + MORE TO READ

Fan Sites

JONAS BROTHERS OFFICIAL SITES
www.jonasbrothers.com
The official site for everything you want to know about all the guys, from tour dates to TV appearances to YouTube clips.

www.myspace.com/jonasbrothers
Want to get really up close and personal with the Jonas Brothers? Head to their MySpace page! You can even leave them a voicemail!

OTHER SITES
http://nickjonline.com
http://www.joe-jonas.com
http://kevinjonasonline.com
www.youtube.com/jonasbrothersmusic

Be Like Them!

The Jonas Brothers are involved in lots of important causes. And you can be, too. Here are just a few examples.

Kids Care Clubs (www.kidscare.org)
See what other kids are up to and how you can start your own group.

The National Wildlife Federation
(www.nwf.org) helps protect all species of animals and the environment.

**The Virtual Volunteering Project
(www.serviceleader.org/vv)** helps people make a difference through the Internet.

YouthNOISE (connected to Save the Children)
(www.youthnoise.com) shows kids how to get involved in volunteering, fund-raising, and making their voices heard.

more to read

Johns, Michael-Anne. *Just Jonas! The Jonas Brothers Up Close and Personal.* New York: Scholastic Inc., 2008. (48 pages)

Mattern, Joanne. *The Jonas Brothers (Robbie Readers).* Hockessin, Del.: Mitchell Lane Publishers, 2008. (32 pages)

Ryals, Lexi. *Jammin' With the Jonas Brothers: An Unauthorized Biography.* New York: Penguin Young Readers Group, 2008. (128 pages)

JONAS BROS.

advocate *noun* a person who supports something or someone

blood sugar *noun* the concentration of glucose, or sugar, in the blood

conventional *adjective* done in a traditional or accepted way

devastated *adjective* shocked and distressed

diabetes *noun* a disease in which the body has trouble controlling the amount of sugar in the blood

executive *noun* someone who has a senior job in a company and is involved in planning its future

Great White Way *noun* since 1901, a nickname for the theater district near Times Square in New York City; the name refers to the area's bright electric lights

hearing impaired *adjective* having limited hearing or no hearing

hormone *noun* a chemical made by the body that helps regulate a particular body function

insulin *noun* a hormone, made by the pancreas, that regulates the amount of sugar in a person's body

mantra *noun* a word or sound repeated to aid in concentration

mesmerizing *adjective* completely absorbing

ministry *noun* organized religious work

moonlighting *verb* working at a second job in addition to one's regular job

nonprofit *adjective* not conducted primarily to make a profit; charities are usually nonprofit organizations

obscurity *noun* the state of being unknown

obsessed *adjective* preoccupied with one thing or person all the time

paparazzi *noun* photographers who pursue celebrities to get photographs of and information about them

promote *verb* to make the public aware of something or someone

propel *verb* to drive or push something forward

publicize *verb* to make known to the public

significant *adjective* important or meaning a great deal

venue *noun* a place where an organized event happens, such as a concert or sporting event

JONAS BROS.

ABOUT THE AUTHOR

Maggie Marron is the author of numerous biographies of pop stars and actors, including Britney Spears, Christina Aguilera, the Backstreet Boys, 'NSync, Will Smith, Jennifer Garner, and many others. She's also interviewed and profiled celebrities for *People* magazine's website, people.com. In addition to her work with celebrities, she's written extensively on a variety of teen topics—from beauty to style to health to dealing with boys—for *CosmoGirl!*. She is currently developing several fiction projects geared toward a teen audience. She lives in New York City with her two cats.